Sports Build Character

FAIRNESS IN SPORTS

by Todd Kortemeier

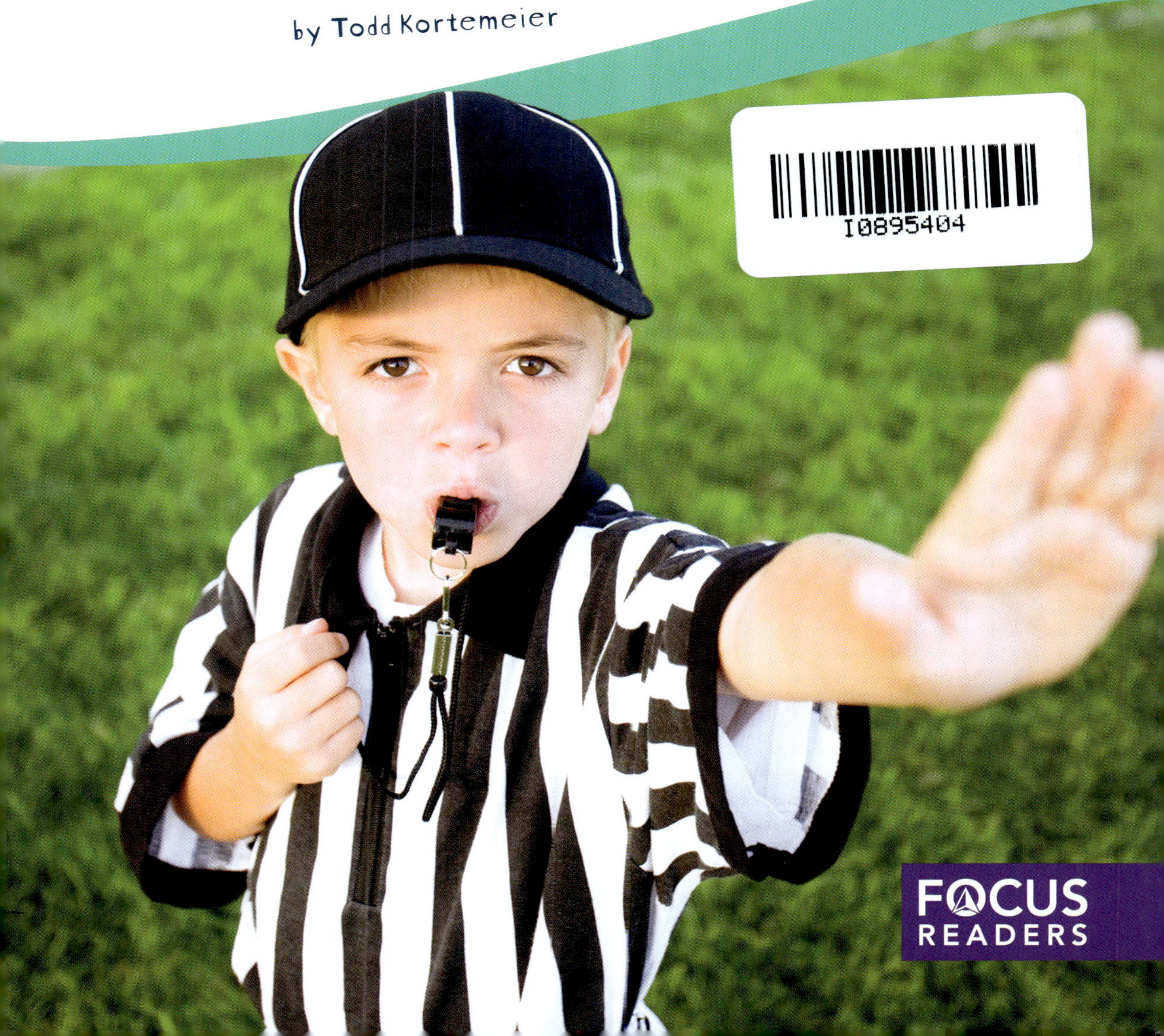

FOCUS READERS

FOCUS READERS

www.focusreaders.com

Focus Readers is distributed by North Star Editions:
sales@northstareditions.com | 888-417-0195

Produced for Focus Readers by Red Line Editorial.

Photographs ©: RichVintage/iStockphoto, cover, 1; buzbuzzer/iStockphoto, 4–5, 29; Nata_Snow/iStockphoto, 7; Greg Baker/AP Images, 8–9; Mark Baker/AP Images, 11; Anthony Correia/Shutterstock Images, 12; Domenico Stinellis/AP Images, 15; David J. Phillip/AP Images, 16; Kevin Frayer/AP Images, 19; Blake Wolf/AP Images, 20; Rawpixel.com/Shutterstock Images, 22–23; legacyimagesphotography/iStockphoto, 25; imtmphoto/iStockphoto, 26–27

ISBN
978-1-63517-532-5 (hardcover)
978-1-63517-604-9 (paperback)
978-1-63517-748-0 (ebook pdf)
978-1-63517-676-6 (hosted ebook)

Library of Congress Control Number: 2017948100

Printed in the United States of America
Mankato, MN
November, 2017

About the Author

Todd Kortemeier is a writer and editor from Minneapolis. He has written more than 50 books for young people, primarily on sports topics.

TABLE OF CONTENTS

57

CHAPTER 1

WHAT IS FAIRNESS?

Knowing right from wrong is a big part of having good character. It is unfair if you know something is wrong but do it anyway. Fairness means doing the right thing. It means showing everyone respect.

The job of a referee is to keep the game fair.

It means not **cheating** to get what you want.

Fairness is very important in sports. A competition has to be fair for everyone to have the same chance of winning. The purpose of sports is to determine the best player or team. If someone cheats, then the result is not fair.

LET'S DISCUSS

In what ways do you try to be fair in daily life?

Runners must run the same distance for a race to be fair.

Sports are more fun when everybody plays fairly. And having fun can be just as important as winning.

CHAPTER 2

FAIRNESS IN ACTION

Dara Torres was one of the fastest swimmers in the United States. She earned a total of 12 Olympic medals. And she made sure she earned each one fairly.

Dara Torres swims in the 50-meter freestyle finals.

Torres was at the 2008 Olympics. The women's 50-meter freestyle race was about to begin. The swimmers waited quietly. Suddenly, Swedish swimmer Therese Alshammar's swimsuit ripped. She was going to miss the race.

Torres's chances at winning were higher if Alshammar did not compete. But Torres wanted a fair win. She asked the officials to delay the race. This allowed Alshammar to change her suit and still swim.

Torres speaks to an official to delay the race.

Torres got her fair win. After the first round, she went on to win the silver medal in the event. She was also given a World Fair Play Award for good **sportsmanship**.

Andy Roddick set a record for the fastest serve in 2004.

In 2005, Andy Roddick was the best American tennis player. He was one of the last 16 players in the Rome Masters **tournament**. Roddick needed just one more point to win his match. It was Fernando Verdasco's turn to **serve**.

Verdasco's first serve was out. He served again. It was also called out. Roddick had won. But he didn't celebrate. Instead, he told the **umpire** that the call was wrong.

Roddick could see the mark the ball made on the court. It had landed in.

So the match continued. Verdasco clawed back to win the game. He went on to win the **set**. Then he won the entire match. Roddick could have kept quiet about the call. He would have won. His fairness had cost him a **trophy** and prize money.

LET'S DISCUSS

If an official misses a call, should a player say anything? Why or why not?

Roddick congratulates Verdasco on his win.

But he chose to do the right thing.

He did not want to win unfairly.

The 2008 Games were Crawford's second time at the Olympics.

Olympic athletes dream of winning a medal. American runner Shawn Crawford thought he had come up just short. He finished fourth in the 200-meter dash at the 2008 Olympics.

But soon after, he learned there had been a mistake. The runners who had finished second and third had been **disqualified**. They ran outside of their lanes. That meant Crawford was a silver medalist.

But Crawford felt uncomfortable accepting his medal. He didn't think he had earned it. He did not think he should get a prize when he really finished fourth.

Crawford saw Churandy Martina at another event a week later. Martina was the second-place runner disqualified at the Olympics.

LET'S DISCUSS

How would you feel if you got an award you did not earn?

It was a close race between Martina (1003) and Crawford (3152).

Crawford boxed up the silver medal and gave it to Martina. Second place still officially belonged to Crawford. But the prize was in the hands of its rightful owner.

The Central Washington players helped their opponent touch each base.

Western Oregon was playing for a spot in the 2008 college softball playoffs. And Sara Tucholsky had just hit a home run. The hit would give the team a 3–0 lead.

In her excitement, Tucholsky forgot to touch first base. She tried to go back, but she hurt her knee. She could not even walk. Her home run would only count if she made it around the bases. Two players from the other team carried Tucholsky. They helped her get the fair win she deserved.

LET'S DISCUSS

Would you help an injured player from the other team? Why or why not?

CHAPTER 3

FAIRNESS AND YOU

Fairness has a place in both life and sports. Everyone does better when they have a fair chance. By being fair, you encourage others to be fair as well.

Sharing the ball with a sibling is one example of fairness.

In many situations, fairness may mean giving up what you want. For example, Shawn Crawford gave up a medal. Fairness may also involve changing how you usually do things. For instance, Sara Tucholsky's opponents did not usually help the other team score a run.

LET'S DISCUSS

How can you tell when someone is treating you fairly?

It is unfair for a swimmer to start before the starting signal.

You can be fair by having an open mind. Fairness happens when people respect one another. In sports, fair play ensures a fair winner. In life, fair actions mean everyone has equal **opportunity**.

ARE YOU FAIR?

Ask yourself these questions and decide.

- Do I treat others how I want to be treated?
- Do I follow the rules?
- Do I speak up if a rule is unfair?
- Do I consider others before I act?
- Do I admit my mistakes?

It's easy to notice when someone treats you unfairly. But challenge yourself to notice when others have been treated unfairly. You could offer a helping hand or a listening ear.

Rules make board games challenging, fun, and fair.

FOCUS ON

FAIRNESS

Write your answers on a separate piece of paper.

1. Write a sentence that describes what was fair about Dara Torres's actions in the swimming competition.

2. Would you have spoken to the umpire if you were Andy Roddick? Why or why not?

3. What event did Shawn Crawford run?

A. 50-meter freestyle

B. marathon

C. 200-meter dash

4. What would have happened if the opposing players hadn't helped Sara Tucholsky reach home plate?

A. She would not have scored a run.

B. She would have to hit again.

C. Her team would have lost automatically.

5. What does **competition** mean in this book?

*Fairness is very important in sports. A **competition** has to be fair for everyone to have the same chance of winning.*

- A. the people who take part in something
- B. a game or contest
- C. something that is hard to do

6. What does **delay** mean in this book?

*She asked the officials to **delay** the race. This allowed Alshammar to change her suit and still swim.*

- A. to do something later
- B. to start something quickly
- C. to make something harder

Answer key on page 32.

GLOSSARY

cheating
Breaking the rules on purpose to gain an advantage.

disqualified
Removed from a competition for breaking a rule.

opportunity
The chance to have or do something.

serve
To deliver the ball in tennis.

set
In tennis, a collection of games that make up a full match.

sportsmanship
Competing in a fair and respectful way.

tournament
A competition that includes many players.

trophy
A prize awarded for certain finishes in a competition.

umpire
A person who is in charge of the rules of a competition.

TO LEARN MORE

BOOKS

Donovan, Sandy. *When Is It My Turn? A Book About Fairness.* Minneapolis: Lerner Publications, 2014.

Herzog, Brad. *Inspiring Stories of Sportsmanship.* Minneapolis: Free Spirit Publishing, 2014.

Raatma, Lucia. *Fairness.* Ann Arbor, MI: Cherry Lake Publishing, 2014.

NOTE TO EDUCATORS

Visit **www.focusreaders.com** to find lesson plans, activities, links, and other resources related to this title.

INDEX

Answer Key: 1. Answers will vary; **2.** Answers will vary; **3.** C; **4.** A; **5.** B; **6.** A